NATURE'S FURY

EARTHQUAKES

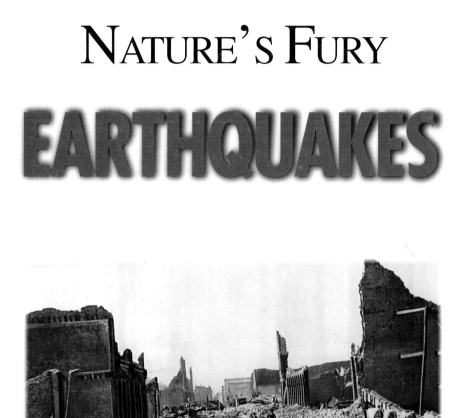

Cari Meister

ABDO
& Daughters

Visit us at
www.abdopub.com

Published by ABDO Publishing Company, 4940 Viking Drive, Edina, MN 55435.
Copyright ©1999 by Abdo Consulting Group, Inc. International copyrights reserved
in all countries. No part of this book may be reproduced in any form without written
permission from the publisher.

Printed in the United States.

Edited by: Paul Joseph
Art Direction: John Hamilton
Contributing Editor: Morgan Hughes

Cover photo: Corbis
Interior photos: AP/Wide World Photos, pages 1, 4, 10, 11, 12, 14, 18
       Corbis, pages 3, 5, 19, 20, 25, 28, 31
       National Oceanic & Atmospheric Administration, pages 21, 22, 23
       United States Geological Survey, page 9, 13, 27

Sources: Lane, Frank W. *The Violent Earth*. Topsfield, Massachusetts: Salem
House, 1986; Laskin, David. *Braving the Elements: The Stormy History of American
Weather*. New York: Doubleday, 1996; Robinson, Andrew. *Earth Shock*. New York:
Thames and Hudson, Ltd, 1993; Various articles on http://www.usatoday.com,
weather section; Wood, Dr. Robert Muir. *Earthquakes and Volcanoes: Causes,
Effects & Predictions*. New York: Weidenfeld & Nicolson, 1987.

Library of Congress Cataloging–in–Publication Data

Meister, Cari.
 Earthquakes / Cari Meister
   p. cm. — (Nature's fury)
 Includes bibliographical references and index.
 Summary: Discusses the nature and measurement of earthquakes and the
devastation that they can cause on land and sea, including the giant seismic waves
known as tsunamis.
 ISBN 1-57765-083-2
 1. Earthquakes—Juvenile literature. 2. Tsunamis—Juvenile literature.
[1. Earthquakes. 2. Tsunamis.] I. Title. II. Series: Meister, Cari. Nature's fury.
QE521.3.M42 1999
551.22—dc21   98-19467
                     CIP
                     AC

CONTENTS

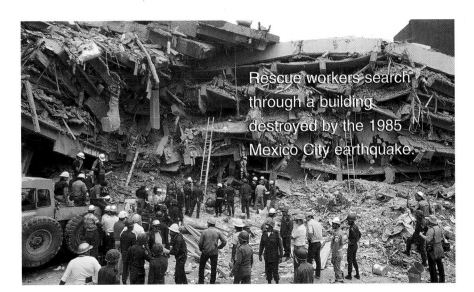

Rescue workers search through a building destroyed by the 1985 Mexico City earthquake.

EARTHQUAKES

IN 1975, PEOPLE IN CHINA WITNESSED SOME VERY strange events. They saw pigs chew off their tails. They found thousands of snakes frozen to death in the snow. Rats appeared from dark holes and stood in the bright daylight. That's not all. It felt as if someone had picked up the province of Liaoning and was gently shaking it.

Pots and jars rattled. Pictures on the walls shook. In one 72-hour period, scientists measured 500 tremors. All of a sudden everything was still. Scientists worried that the tremors meant that something much bigger was coming. They ordered approximately three million people from their homes.

Parts of Kobe, Japan, burn after an earthquake strikes the city in 1995.

bigger. They were the sign of an earthquake. On February 4, the earthquake came. The earth shook with great vigor. Roads folded. Many homes crumbled. Streams of water shot up from the ground. Towns were destroyed. Tragically, 300 people lost their lives. But it could have been much worse. The people were lucky. They were warned.

The scientists were right. The tremors were a sign of something

Toppled buildings from
the devastating 1985
Mexico City earthquake.

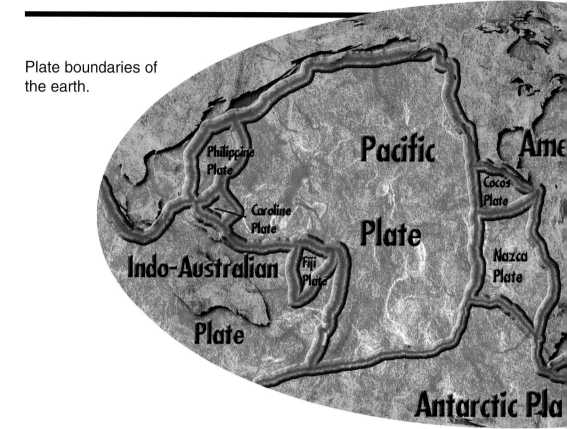

Plate boundaries of the earth.

Philippine Plate

Pacific

Ame

Cocos Plate

Caroline Plate

Plate

Nazca Plate

Indo-Australian

Fiji Plate

Plate

Antarctic Pla

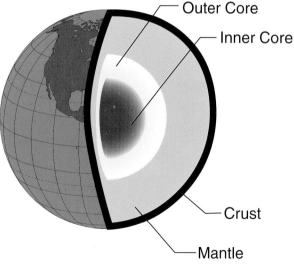

Outer Core

Inner Core

Crust

Mantle

Cross-section of the earth.

Earthquakes are hard to predict. Even today, scientists do not have a foolproof method of predicting earthquakes. Some scientists believe that animals give clues to earthquakes, like the pigs in China. But not all scientists agree. Earthquakes can come suddenly, without any warning. Or they can not come at all, even when scientists are convinced that they will.

We think of the ground as solid and unshakable. It's easy to be-

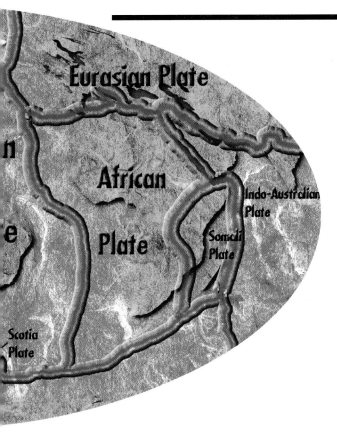

Eurasian Plate

African

Indo-Australian
Plate

Somali
Plate

Plate

Scotia
Plate

into smaller pieces. You can see where most of the pieces would fit if you could put them back together. But there are spots where the pieces don't quite match up because some very small pieces crumbled away. Now imagine wrapping the peanut brittle pieces you have left around a ball. The pieces of peanut brittle are kind of like the earth's outer shell. The earth's rocky crust is broken up into big pieces called plates. The plates are made up of crust and of rock from the upper mantle. Below the plates, hot rock churns, so hot that it is not solid. The plates float on this hot rock.

The plates are always moving. They don't move fast. They usually move about two to three inches (5 to 8 cm) a year. The plates carry whatever is on top of them. They carry continents, islands, and oceans. When the plates move, they bump into each other. Sometimes they drift apart or pass each other sideways. Sometimes the plates push against each other so hard that pressure builds. When the pressure is finally relieved, we feel an earthquake.

lieve this because we rarely see or feel that it's moving. But it does.

The earth has three main layers. Think about a golf ball. If you peel away the outer layer, there is another layer. If you peel away this layer, there is yet another layer. The earth is similar. Underneath the oceans and soil there is a layer called the crust. It is made up of rock. Underneath the crust is the mantle. Underneath the mantle is the core.

Think of the crust as one large piece of peanut brittle broken up

PREDICTING EARTHQUAKES

EARTHQUAKES HAVE RAVAGED THE EARTH FOR A LONG time. People from all over the world have come up with stories explaining earthquakes. Some people believe that an earthquake is a punishment sent by God. In Hindu folklore, the violent shaking means a giant elephant is shaking its head. The Greeks blamed their sea god, Poseidon. In Japanese folklore, *Namazu* is to blame. *Namazu* is a giant catfish that is said to live below the earth's sur-face. *Namazu* is kept under control by a god. When the god falls asleep, the giant catfish thrashes around, causing earthquakes.

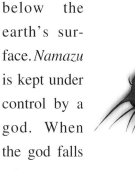

Namazu

Scientists do not know exactly what causes earthquakes. They know that earthquakes occur when plates collide and shift. But the plates are always shifting. Some-times when the plates move in a certain way, there is an earthquake. Sometimes there is not. Because scientists can not always pinpoint *why* an earthquake happens, it is difficult for them to tell *when* one will occur.

Scientists do know a lot of other things about earthquakes. They know that earthquakes usually occur near where they have occurred before. Some areas of the world are more prone to earthquakes than other areas. Japan has more earthquakes than any other place on earth and the most deadly. About 1,000 earth-quakes are felt in Japan every year.

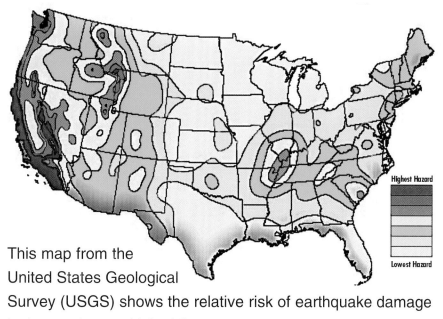

This map from the United States Geological Survey (USGS) shows the relative risk of earthquake damage in the contiguous United States.

In the United States, California gets a lot of earthquakes.

Earthquakes usually occur near fault lines. A fault is a place where the crust has broken. Think back to the peanut brittle. A fault would be the space between two pieces of peanut brittle. We can see some faults on earth. Some people say that the San Andreas Fault in California looks like a big, puckered scar. We cannot see all of the earth's faults. Some faults are hidden deep below the earth's surface. Some are even under the ocean floor!

Some faults have been around for millions of years. Other faults are in the process of forming. Forces deep inside the earth make the rocky parts of the crust and mantle bend. When the pressure becomes too great, the rock snaps. The snap, or split, of the rock creates a fault. Scientists study the areas around faults, like Japan and California, to learn more about earthquakes.

Seismologists are scientists who study earthquakes. They have special tools called seismographs to help them gather information about earthquakes. A seismograph records seismic waves. Seismic waves are energy waves created by an earthquake. Seismic waves form concentric circles of energy around the focus. The focus is the spot where a rocky plate breaks beneath the earth's surface. Seismic waves tell seismologists what is going on underneath the surface. Seismographs are important in locating an earthquake's epicenter. The epicenter is the place where the earthquake is the strongest and most dangerous. Sometimes seismographs help scientists predict an earthquake. Usually, an exact time frame is impossible.

There are three parts to a seismograph. A weight attached to a wire or spring senses seismic waves. A pen records the information. In between the wire and the pen is a system that changes the waves to a form that scientists can read. Some seismographs are computer operated.

A scientist measures the strength of an earthquake with a seismograph.

MEASURING EARTHQUAKES

SOME EARTHQUAKES DESTROY BUILDINGS, HIGHWAYS and homes. Other earthquakes just shake the pictures on walls. Many earthquakes are so small, or so far below the earth's surface that they go unnoticed. How violent the earth shakes depends on the focus location. If an earthquake's focus is deep in the earth, it will usually cause less damage than if the focus is closer to the surface.

Seismic waves also affect how much the earth shakes during an

A bank building damaged by an earthquake in 1995 in Kobe, Japan.

earthquake. There are two kinds of seismic waves: body waves and surface waves. Body waves start at the focus and travel out. Surface waves travel along the earth's surface. They travel away from the epicenter. Surface waves sometimes make the ground feel as if it's rolling. Surface waves cause the most damage to buildings, roads, and bridges.

As you learned in the last chapter, seismologists use seismographs to record earthquake waves. The seismograph's pen records seismic waves by drawing lines. When a wave is closer, or stronger, the line is longer. When a seismic wave is farther away, or weaker, the line

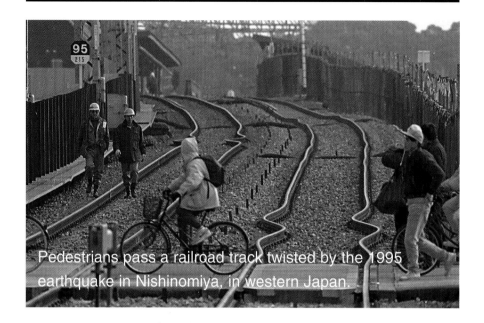

Pedestrians pass a railroad track twisted by the 1995 earthquake in Nishinomiya, in western Japan.

is shorter. Seismographs help scientists measure an earthquake.

Scientists use other tools to measure an earthquake's intensity and magnitude. Intensity measures the damage that people can see and feel. Did roads buckle? Did buildings fall? Did dishes rattle? Intensity is not measured by a scientific instrument. Intensity is measured by what people say. After an earthquake, workers at the National Earthquake Center in Colorado find eye-witnesses. They mail questionnaires to people about the earthquake. They mail questionnaires to people near the earthquake's epicenter. They also mail questionnaires to people farther away

from the epicenter. After the people respond, seismologists make a map of the area. The map shows locations and intensities based on how people responded.

Intensity is sometimes hard to measure. Some people may look at a crumpled building and say the damage is severe. Other people might look at the same building and say the damage is moderate. In 1902, Giuseppe Mercalli invented a scale to help measure intensity. The Mercalli Intensity Scale gave different numbers for different degrees of damage. For example, an earthquake was given the number one if it was not felt at all. It was given a two if it was felt indoors by some people. The higher the number, the more severe the earthquake. The scale gave scientists a way to compare earthquakes. As the years went on, building methods changed. Scientists updated the Mercalli scale to include new types of construction. Today, the intensity scale is called the Modified Mercalli Intensity Scale.

Magnitude is the measurement of an earthquake's strength. Scientists use two scales to measure magnitude: the Richter scale and the moment magnitude scale. The Richter scale, invented by Charles Richter in 1935, gives an earthquake a number based on how much the ground shakes. The higher the number, the more severe the earthquake. Today, more scientists use the moment magnitude scale, which measures how rocks move in an earthquake.

The twentieth century's 10 most powerful earthquakes, according to the United States Geological Survey.

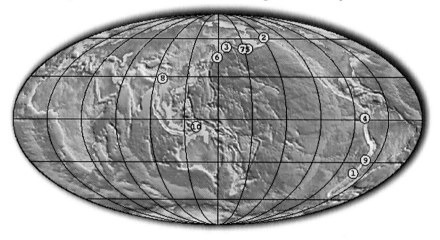

	Date	Magnitude on the Richter scale
1.) Chile	05/22/1960	9.5 Mw
2.) Alaska	03/28/1964	9.2 Mw
3.) Russia	11/04/1952	9.0 Mw
4.) Ecuador	01/31/1906	8.8 Mw
5.) Alaska	03/09/1957	8.8 Mw
6.) Kuril Islands	11/06/1958	8.7 Mw
7.) Alaska	02/04/1965	8.7 Mw
8.) India	08/15/1950	8.6 Mw
9.) Argentina	11/11/1922	8.5 Mw
10.) Indonesia	02/01/1938	8.5 Mw

FAMOUS EARTHQUAKES

ON APRIL 18, 1906, JUST after 5:00 a.m., thousands of people in San Francisco, California, jumped from their beds. The ground shook. The cupboards rattled. Furniture skidded along the floor. Mothers and fathers gathered their children and ran outside. They didn't even have time to change out of their pajamas! The streets of San Francisco were filled with terrified people watching walls and ceilings crash to the ground. Three times the ground rumbled. Then all was quiet. At first, the people sighed with relief. Then they watched in horror. The city was on fire!

Red-hot flames tore through the city. Sharp orange daggers of fire devoured building after building. In two days, the fires destroyed 500 city blocks. Buildings and homes were only charred remains.

San Francisco stood draped in black. When it was over 700 people had died and 28,000 buildings were destroyed.

The fires were caused by overturned stoves. When the earthquake shook, wood and coal stoves tipped over, spilling flames. The fire department tried to hush the flames, but they didn't have enough water. The earthquake had torn open the main water lines. When fire fighters went to the hydrants, no water came.

The Winchester Hotel burns after the San Francisco earthquake of April 18, 1906.

Inside an Earthquake

Earth's crust is made of many huge plates, which often slide past each other on a fault line. Sometimes the edges of two plates get stuck. Pressure builds.

16

Finally, the two plates quickly slip past each other along the fault line. The plates can lurch forward several feet (several meters), producing a severe earthquake and causing much destruction in populated areas.

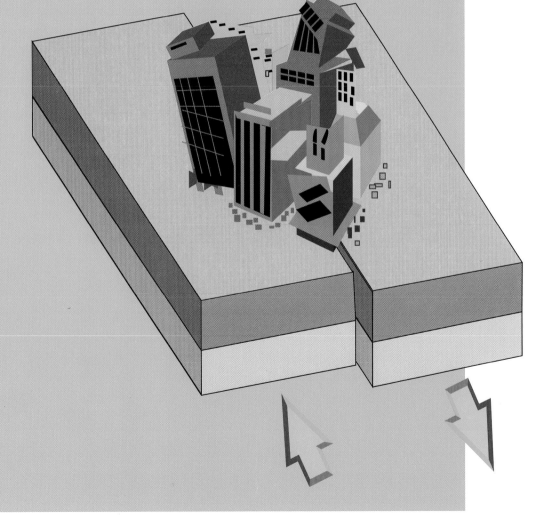

About 80 years later, this time in Mexico City, another early morning earthquake shook people from bed. On September 19, 1985, just before 7:30 a.m., huge vibrations shook the city. In minutes, part of the city was destroyed. Nearly 7,000 buildings were damaged. The most horrifying scenes were near where tall buildings once stood. Some people were out walking the early morning streets. They screamed as they watched layer after layer of tall buildings fall. Hospitals, apartment buildings, schools, and businesses crumbled into rubble. Falling buildings crushed over 10,000 people. It took days to find the bodies among the rubble.

Kobe, Japan -1995.

In 1995, an earthquake killed 5,000 people in Kobe, Japan. After the earthquake, newspapers showed the dead wrapped in blankets. Not only did the earthquake violently shake the city, it brought over 600 aftershocks. An aftershock is a tremor that occurs after an earthquake. Aftershocks are less powerful than earthquake shakes, but they are still frightening and dangerous.

Most earthquakes occur along fault lines. But not always. In 1811 and 1812, three earthquakes struck Missouri. The first one struck on December 16, 1811. People rushed out of their cabins at 2:00 a.m. Witnesses said that the air smelled of sulfur. The skies flashed light. They watched as parts of the forests crashed to the ground. They saw huge cracks in the earth open up. The second wave began on January 23, 1812. The third earthquake struck Missouri on February 7, 1812. It was the most frightening and strongest of the three. The February 7 earthquake was felt all the way in Washington, D.C.!

Missouri is not near any visible fault lines. It is earthquakes like these that really puzzle scientists.

Rescue workers pull a body out of a building demolished by the 1985 Mexico City earthquake.

The result of a tsunami in Hilo, Hawaii, 1960.

TSUNAMI!

DEEP DOWN ON THE OCEAN FLOOR, THERE ARE FAULT lines. Just like fault lines on land, fault lines on the ocean floor trigger earthquakes. Earthquakes under the oceans sometimes start tsunamis. A tsunami is a giant seismic sea wave. Tsunami is Japanese for "large waves in the harbor."

Tsunamis start when an earthquake disrupts the ocean floor. Holes open. Rocks move. When the earthquake rumbles the ocean floor, a large mound of water forms on the ocean surface. In a short time, the mound changes into wide, low waves. The waves travel fast. They travel about 500 miles (805 km) per hour! At this time, the waves are about two to three feet (.6 to .9 meters) high.

Kodiak, Alaska, 1963

Some waves stay out at sea and never hit land. Some waves grow to enormous heights and level entire coastal towns. If a tsunami approaches your town, watch out!

When tsunami waves hit land, they are no longer just two to three feet (.6 to .9 meters) high.

In May 1960, tsunami waves battered southern Chile, killing 2,000 people. Waves in Hawaii reached 65 feet (20 m). The waves flattened the city of Hilo. Buildings were crushed. Parking meters were bent over. The tsunami claimed 61 lives in Hawaii, 100 more in Japan, and 20 in the Philippines.

How can a series of waves two to three feet (.6 to .9 meters) high get so big? Here's how: As a tsunami comes closer to land, the water gets shallower and shallower. The front part of the wave slows down. The back part of the wave pushes forward. The back part of the wave builds up on the front part of the wave. The build-up forms a giant wall of water. When the wall breaks, the water crashes into land.

Some tsunamis crush everything in their way. Some tsunamis carry things like boats out to sea, only to hurl them back minutes later. Some tsunamis produce waves that pull up buildings and houses from the ground. It's hard to know how a tsunami will act.

Always remember that tsunamis come in waves. Many people have died, thinking it safe to return home after one wave. Don't think it's safe after one wave crashes into shore. Another wave may be on its way.

Often, an earthquake in one part of the world triggers tsunamis all over the world. The Hilo tsunami was a result of an earthquake

A chart from the National Oceanic & Atmospheric Administration (NOAA) showing the time it would take for a tsunami to reach various spots in the Pacific Ocean after an earthquake centered in the Hawaiian Islands.

A man in the lower left of this photo watches helplessly as a giant wave engulfs the city of Hilo, Hawaii, on April 1, 1946. It was the Hawaiian Islands' worst-ever natural disaster, with 159 people losing their lives. The man on the pier was never seen again.

in Chile. The earthquake in Chile also triggered tsunamis on two Japanese islands.

People in Anchorage, Alaska, suffered both an earthquake and a tsunami in 1964. The earthquake was so powerful that it ripped a mountain in two. An entire movie theater fell into a 30-foot (9-m) deep hole. Railroad tracks twisted. Houses fell into the sea. When the rumbling stopped, people thought they were safe. They weren't. The earthquake triggered a tsunami. Houses were crushed under heavy waves. People drowned. The earthquake had far-reaching effects. Huge waves crashed into coastal towns all the way from Alaska to California!

THE SAN ANDREAS FAULT

THE SAN ANDREAS FAULT IS ONE OF THE BIGGEST FAULTS in the world. It's where two large plates—the American plate and the Pacific plate—grind up against each other. The San Andreas Fault is partly on land and partly beneath the sea. On land, it runs from the Gulf of California, past Los Angeles and San Francisco up to Cape Mendocino.

From here, it goes back to sea. Areas around the San Andreas Fault have a lot of earthquake activity.

The big earthquake in San Francisco in 1906 was a result of the San Andreas Fault. Since then, more earthquakes have struck, but none as violent. In October 1989, another earthquake struck the San Francisco area, killing 62 people. A large part of the Bay Bridge collapsed. The bridge crushed cars. Scientists are watching and waiting for more earthquakes to come. They are sure that they will. The movement in the rocks tells them that it is only a matter of time.

If you visit California you can see the San Andreas Fault. It is a big gap in the earth's crust. In some places the gap is a few hundred feet wide. In other areas it is wider than a mile. As you learned before, the earth's plates are always moving. In some parts of California, the fault moves north at about an inch per year. You can see this happening. Look at the roads. Look at fences. If the lines don't match up, it's because the plates are moving.

Sometimes the plates move smoothly past one another. Sometimes they don't. When they do not

The Carrizo Plains provide good visibility of the San Andreas Fault in southern California.

California

San Andreas Fault

Citrus Heights
Santa Rosa
Napa
Fairfield
Sacramento
Stockton
Oakland
San Francisco
Modesto
Palo Alto
San Jose
Salinas
Fresno
Bakersfield
Santa Barbara
Oxnard
San Bernardino
Anaheim
Oceanside

move smoothly, the edges of the plates lock together. It gets very tight until finally a rock snaps. Then a small earthquake occurs. In Hollister, California, this happens often. Scientists don't worry about places like these along the fault. Small earthquakes relieve pressure. The more small earthquakes there are, the less likely a huge earthquake will occur.

Scientists do worry about other places along the fault. They especially worry about places along the fault that have not moved. When there is no movement, pressure builds. When small earthquakes don't relieve the pressure, pressure just continues to build. The more pressure that builds, the more violent the earthquake will be. Scientists are especially worried about the Los Angeles and San Francisco areas. Los Angeles and San Francisco are both very big cities. There are a lot of tall buildings. If a big earthquake came, many people would die. Most people would die from falling debris from tall buildings, highways, bridges, and other human-made structures.

STAYING SAFE

EARTHQUAKES ARE HARD TO PREDICT. WE NEVER REALLY know when one may strike. It is best to always be ready, especially in areas around the San Andreas Fault. If you are inside during an earthquake, cover yourself with something strong. A table, or other big piece of furniture may save you from falling debris.

If there is no strong furniture, find a doorway. Stand in the doorway frame. Doorways provide protection from falling walls. Never go near windows or mirrors. You may be cut by glass. Never ride in an elevator during an earthquake. Cables may snap, dropping the elevator car! After the earthquake has stopped shaking, get out of the building! The earthquake may have weakened the walls. It may crumble after the earthquake is done, or during an aftershock.

If you are outside during an earthquake, stay away from buildings, power lines, highway overpasses and anything else that may fall. If you are in a car, have the driver stop. Pull off the road in a safe place. Stay inside the car. The car may give you protection from falling objects.

More people die from earthquake-related accidents than from the actual shaking itself. In the great San Francisco earthquake of 1906, 90 percent of the people who died were killed from related accidents. Fire and falling buildings caused the most deaths.

An apartment building damaged by the 1994 Northridge, California, earthquake.

One way to lessen earthquake deaths is to find better ways of building. Architects and scientists are working together to build houses and buildings that can stand up to earthquakes. Today, buildings are built to sway during an earthquake, so they won't crumble as easily. They also have more steel to make them stronger.

Some buildings have special computer sensors. The computer sensors adjust the weight of a building when the ground shakes. This is how it works:

1) A moveable weight rests on the top of the building.

2) Special motion sensors tell the computer when the building is vibrating.

3) The computer calculates how the weight has to shift to balance the vibrations.

4) The weight on the top of the building moves to where the computer tells it to go.

There are some things you can do in your home to reduce earthquake damage. Never put heavy objects on high shelves. Put heavy objects near the floor. This way they don't have far to fall. Bolt bookcases to wooden posts inside the walls. This way they are less likely to crash down on you. Make sure that there are secure latches on closet and cabinet doors. Earthquakes do happen. There is no way to stop them. It is best to be prepared.

A fire burns out of control after the 1989 San Francisco earthquake.

INTERNET SITES

http://www.usatoday.com

Go to WEATHER. Check out more about earthquakes, tsunamis and more!

http://earthquake.usgs.gov

The National Earthquake Information Center's official Web site. Search the database, get current earthquake information or see a map of the 10 largest earthquakes of the century.

http://home.earthlink.net/~torg/ca.hmtl

See what other kids have to say about earthquakes, look at kids' drawings of earthquakes and more!

These sites are subject to change. Go to your favorite search engine and type in "earthquakes" for more sites.

PASS IT ON

Science buffs: educate readers around the country by passing on information you've learned about earthquakes. Share your little-known facts and interesting stories. We want to hear from you!

To get posted on the ABDO Publishing Company Web site, E-mail us at "Science@abdopub.com"

Visit the ABDO Publishing Company Web site at:
www.abdopub.com

GLOSSARY

Aftershock: A small earthquake that occurs after a larger earthquake.

Body waves: Energy waves that travel out from the focus of an earthquake to the earth's surface.

Concentric: Rings that move out from one point.

Epicenter: The part of the earth's surface directly above the focus of an earthquake.

Eyewitness: A person who sees an event first-hand.

Fault: A deep crack in the earth.

Focus: The spot inside the earth where the rock first breaks during an earthquake.

Intensity: A measurement of the movement and damage caused by an earthquake, measured by what people felt and saw.

Magnitude: A measurement of an earthquake's strength based on how much the ground shook.

Moment magnitude scale: A scale used to measure an earthquake's strength.

Plates: Pieces of the earth's top layer.

Richter scale: A scale used to measure an earthquake's strength.

Seismic waves: Energy waves released during earthquakes.

Seismograph: A tool used to measure ground movement.

Seismologists: Scientists who study earthquakes.

Tsunamis: Large seismic sea waves.

Surface waves: Energy waves that travel away from an earthquake's epicenter on the earth's surface.

The Bay Bridge was heavily damaged after the 1989 San Francisco earthquake.

INDEX

Survivors walk amidst the ruins after the 1906 San Francisco earthquake.